CW00871830

CHINA'S
TIANZI MOUNTAIN

by Debbie Vilardi

abdobooks.com

Published by Pop!, a division of ABDO, PO Box 398166,
Minneapolis, Minnesota 55439. Copyright © 2021 by POP, LLC.
International copyrights reserved in all countries. No part
of this book may be reproduced in any form without written
permission from the publisher. Pop!™ is a trademark and logo
of POP, LLC.

Printed in the United States of America, North Mankato,
Minnesota.

102020
012021

THIS BOOK CONTAINS
RECYCLED MATERIALS

Cover Photo: iStockphoto
Interior Photos: iStockphoto, 1, 6, 8, 9, 25, 26, 28, 29; Shutterstock
Images, 5, 7, 11, 12, 13, 14–15, 17, 18, 21, 22–23, 27; Science Stock
Photography/Science Source, 20

Editor: Alyssa Krekelberg
Series Designers: Candice Keimig, Victoria Bates, and Laura
Graphenteen

Library of Congress Control Number: 2020940280

Publisher's Cataloging-in-Publication Data

Names: Vilardi, Debbie, author.

Title: China's Tianzi Mountain / by Debbie Vilardi

Description: Minneapolis, Minnesota : POP!, 2021 | Series:
  Nature's mysteries | Includes online resources and index

Identifiers: ISBN 9781532169175 (lib. bdg.) | ISBN 9781532169533
  (ebook)

Subjects: LCSH: Tianzi Mountain (China)--Juvenile literature.
  | Mountains--Juvenile literature. | Geologic erosion--
  Juvenile literature. | Curiosities and wonders--Juvenile
  literature. | Mystery--Juvenile literature. | Geography--
  Juvenile literature.

Classification: DDC 910.02--dc23

WELCOME TO
DiscoverRoo!

Pop open this book and you'll find QR codes loaded

with information, so you can learn even more!

Scan this code* and others like

it while you read, or visit the

website below to make this

book pop!

popbooksonline.com/tianzi-mountain

*Scanning QR codes requires a web-enabled smart device with a QR code reader app and a camera.

TABLE OF CONTENTS

CHAPTER 1

GOING UP THE MOUNTAIN

A **cable car** rises in the air and passes through a thin mist. It is going up a mountain. The people inside the car look around. They can see **pillars** of stone that rise from the ground like castle towers.

WATCH A VIDEO HERE!

The cable cars at Tianzi Mountain have large windows on each side. Visitors can look out at the scenery as they ride.

The car goes higher and higher. Soon, it's

at the top of Tianzi Mountain.

FUN FACT The cable car ride to the top of Tianzi Mountain takes 6 minutes and 44 seconds.

Tianzi Mountain is a 4,140-foot-(1,262 m) tall pillar. The area around it has more than 3,000 similar rock pillars. But Tianzi Mountain is the tallest point. The pillars are in China.

The top of Tianzi Mountain gives visitors a great view of the other stone pillars and the surrounding landscape.

WHERE IS TIANZI MOUNTAIN?

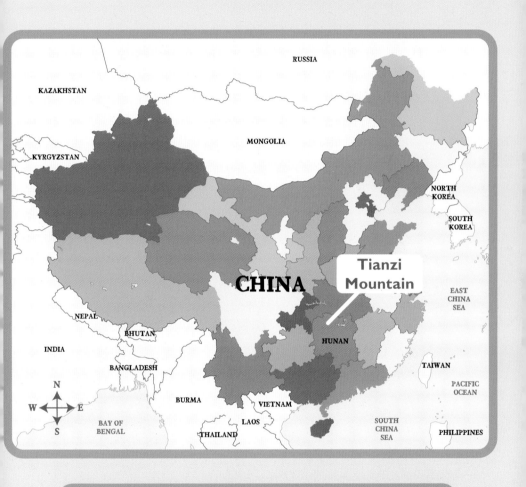

Tianzi Mountain is in the Zhangjiajie National Forest Park. This park is in an area of China called Hunan.

The pillars inspired the fantasy world in the popular movie Avatar.

Some scientists think Tianzi Mountain could be 300 million years old. The mountain and the other rock pillars got their unique shapes after being hit with wind and water for years.

Some people who visit the strange stone pillars feel like they've stepped onto a different planet.

CHAPTER 2

THE MOUNTAIN FORMS

If people look closely, they can see stripes on Tianzi Mountain. These stripes are different rock layers. They formed millions of years ago. Back then, the area looked very different. There were no **pillars**. Instead, there was a large ocean.

LEARN MORE HERE!

The rock pillars near Tianzi Mountain have layers with various colors and shapes.

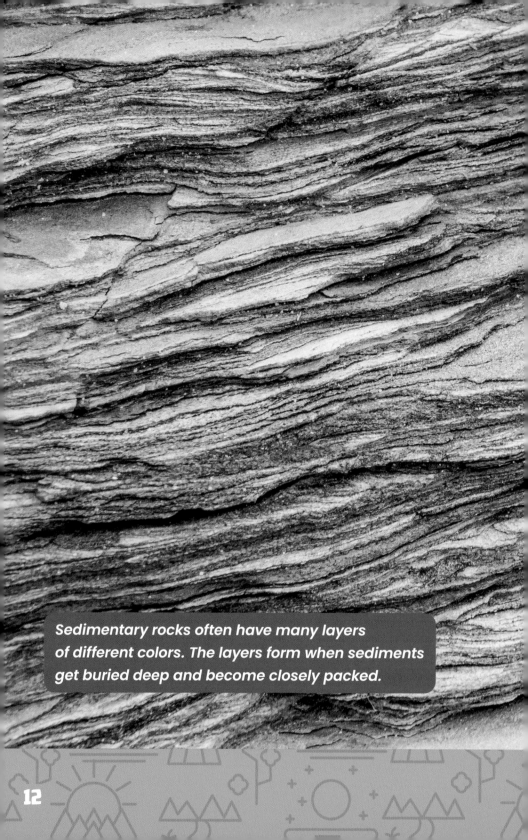

Sedimentary rocks often have many layers of different colors. The layers form when sediments get buried deep and become closely packed.

The rock layers formed at different times. They tell scientists about the history of the area. Layers of sand and shells rested on the ocean floor. These layers hardened into **sedimentary rocks**.

ROCKS AND MINERALS

Tianzi Mountain has different kinds of sedimentary rocks. Limestone formed from the shells of sea creatures. Sandstone formed from the sand. The sandstone held a **mineral** called quartz. Quartz is a common mineral that forms crystals.

Millions of years ago, pieces of Earth's crust crashed into each other. This can cause the landscape to rise. This may be what created the Tianzi Mountain area. But scientists are still studying it.

A crash of land masses also formed the Himalayas. These mountains are the highest in the world.

FUN FACT

There are legends about how the stone pillars formed. One story says that the pillars are the writing brushes of a leader who died.

CHAPTER 3

SHAPING THE PILLARS

It took millions of years for the mountains to become **pillars**. Over time, the mountains experienced **weathering**. Weathering broke parts of the rock.

For example, plant roots grew into holes.

COMPLETE AN ACTIVITY HERE!

When the roots grew, they cracked rock.

Rain and wind cause weathering too.

Strong tree roots can help shape an area of land.

A river's water carries away bits of soil and rock. This process gradually changes the shape of its banks.

Erosion also helped form the pillars.

Erosion happens when rock is moved

by wind or water. Wind blows rock pieces

away. Water carries them to rivers.

This process has been happening to the

pillars for more than 300 million years.

FUN FACT

Erosion happens at different rates on different spots. That's what causes the pillars to have uneven ledges and a jagged look.

The types of rocks found on Tianzi

Mountain and the surrounding pillars

have affected how the area looks.

For example, quartz sandstone resists

weathering. The peaks around Tianzi

Quartz sandstone is a hard material.

Limestone forms in warm, shallow water. So, geologists know cliffs that have limestone in them were once in water.

Mountain are mostly quartz sandstone.

But the bases are soft limestone.

Limestone experiences weathering more

quickly than other types of rocks.

WEATHERING, EROSION, AND DEPOSITION

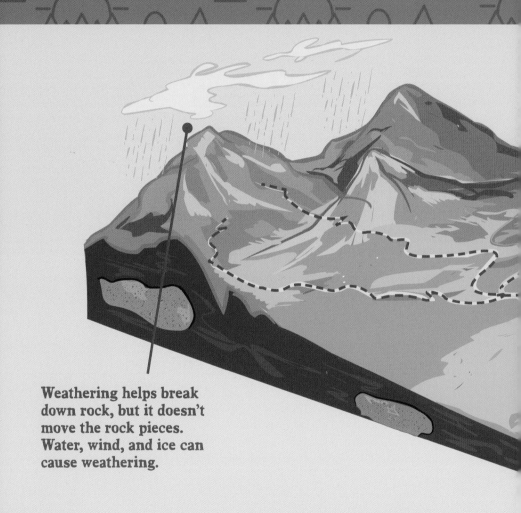

Weathering helps break down rock, but it doesn't move the rock pieces. Water, wind, and ice can cause weathering.

Weathering, erosion, and deposition do different things to rocks.

Erosion takes the pieces away. Gravity, ice, water, and wind cause erosion.

Deposition is when the rock pieces are dropped in a new spot. This can create things such as sand dunes.

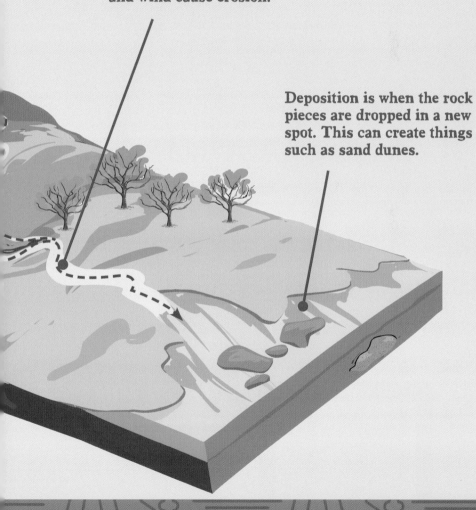

CHAPTER 4

EFFECTS OF TOURISM

There are many cracks in Tianzi Mountain and the other **pillars**. Dirt has filled these cracks. This has allowed plants to grow there. There are also caves at the bases of some pillars. There is a lot of wildlife in the area.

LEARN MORE HERE!

People can see macaque monkeys on Tianzi Mountain when the area isn't too busy. Otherwise, the monkeys will hide.

FUN FACT

The Chinese giant salamander lives at the base of the pillars. Monkeys and birds live in the area too.

People say the best time to visit Tianzi Mountain is in the spring and fall.

The Tianzi Mountain area is a popular place for **tourists**. Visitors use paths to walk up the mountain. People used to stay in hotels and ate in restaurants in the area. All of this activity disturbed plants and animals. Tourists also left trash behind.

Tourists gather at the base of the mountain before heading up.

China began taking steps to protect the area. Some of the buildings were removed. And a tall elevator was added so fewer people would use the trails.

The elevator was completed in 2002.

The pillars are constantly changing through weathering and erosion. But people can do their part to slow down human-caused erosion.

This keeps tourists away from the plants and animals. People hope the area's amazing rock pillars will stay safe for many more years.

MAKING CONNECTIONS

TEXT-TO-SELF

Would you want to ride the elevator to the top of Tianzi Mountain? Why or why not?

TEXT-TO-TEXT

Have you read other books about weathering or erosion? What did you learn?

TEXT-TO-WORLD

Do you think tourists should be allowed to visit natural areas such as Tianzi Mountain? Why or why not?

GLOSSARY

cable car — a vehicle that is attached to an overhead cable and moved up and down a set path.

mineral — a nonliving solid that forms naturally.

pillar — a tall vertical structure.

sedimentary rock — a type of rock formed when smaller rock fragments are pressed together over time.

tourist — someone who visits a place for enjoyment.

weathering — the breaking up of material by weather and other conditions in the environment.

INDEX

ONLINE RESOURCES

popbooksonline.com

Scan this code* and others like it while you read, or visit the website below to make this book pop!

popbooksonline.com/tianzi-mountain

*Scanning QR codes requires a web-enabled smart device with a QR code reader app and a camera.